The 30-Minute Guide to
Talent and Succession Management

A Quick Reference Guide for Business Leaders

Doris Sims Spies, SPHR

Published by Talent Benchstrength Solutions 2017

ISBN: 978-0-692-91364-2

Cover Art by Jeremy H. Sims

Editorial Review by Julie Rael and Spencer F. Sims

Talent Benchstrength® 2013 by Doris Sims Spies

Any people depicted in stock imagery provided by Thinkstock are models, and such images are being used for illustrative purposes only. Certain stock imagery © by Thinkstock.

To order additional copies with a volume discount, or to obtain customized versions of this book, contact Doris Sims Spies, SPHR at 214-906-3155 or doris@talentbenchstrength.com.

www.TalentBenchstrength.com

Talent Benchstrength Solutions
Succession and Talent Reviews

Preface

Talent benchstrength is a critical strategic and risk management function in today's workplace. Why is your talent benchstrength so important when there are so many business priorities? If you think about it, if you are able to identify, to develop and to retain top talent, and you provide an environment that fosters engagement and productivity, EVERYTHING else you are striving to achieve for your organization will naturally follow.

> In today's world, the talent in our organization is a **key differentiator**. Our talent creates our solutions, our products and our services. Our talent serves our customers, and manages the important work of the organization **every day**.

The purpose of this book is to provide practical advice and explanations to help business leaders learn more about Talent Benchstrength strategy, and to identify and develop high performing employees, high potential employees, key experts and successors. This book is designed to answer common questions business leaders have about talent benchstrength and succession planning. It has been created as a quick reference guide that leaders can read in 30 minutes to increase understanding about the growing importance of developing talent and successors.

I have a passion for corporate talent benchstrength because it is a win for the company and a win for employees. What if all organizations spent the same level of time and energy on talent planning and development as they currently spend on budgeting processes? Both processes are critical projections of the future needs of the organization, to achieve the strategy and business goals. The most successful organizations identify and develop BOTH the talent resources and the financial resources to create, sell and support the organization's products and services.

This book does not provide legal advice. Business leaders and their Human Resource partners are advised to work with professional legal counsel to review and approve all talent assessment, succession planning, and high potential identification and development strategic plans, processes and programs created and implemented within their own organization.

To be successful, the organization needs the best resources and talent to lead the way. The vision of this book is to inspire you to develop all talent in the organization, and to continuously identify and focus attention and resources on the "point-in-time" talented people who are ready and able to achieve more, both for their own career and for the organization.

Doris Sims Spies, SPHR

A Talent Benchstrength strategy is NOT like a box of chocolates…you should <u>always know</u> the talent you have and the talent you need to get to achieve your goals.

Doris Sims Spies, SPHR

Key Points and Where to Find Them

Key Points and Where to Find Them (Continued)

Chapter One
What is a Talent Benchstrength Strategy?

Building a strong talent benchstrength foundation is similar to building a strong financial foundation in the organization—to create a sustainable and successful business, an organization must develop and retain **top talent** as well as a **positive cash flow**.

> **Building and maintaining a strong Talent Benchstrength**SM **strategy is a** *proactive* **way to protect the company from talent loss, and to identify talent resources needed to achieve business goals.**
>
> **A talent benchstrength strategy is designed to retain high performing and high potential employees by actively developing competencies and career path options.**

The <u>objectives</u> of a Talent Benchstrength strategy include:

- Identification of successor candidates to fill high vacancy risk jobs and future leadership roles

- Development of knowledge, skills and abilities to help prepare employees for future roles in the organization

- Retention of top talent and knowledge within the organization

- Increasing diversity within the top talent and leadership populations of the organization

- Developing more cross-functional career movement and job experiences in the organization, to increase the "storehouse" of knowledge and skills in the company and to increase the flexibility of employees to take on a variety of job roles and responsibilities

Why Is an Internal Talent Benchstrength Strategy Important?

In today's world, your talent is a key differentiator between your company and your competitors' companies. Your talent creates your products and services, serves your customers, and manages the important business of your organization every day—what could be more important than focusing on the retention and development of your top talent?

This is why top companies know:

We need a *budget process* to identify financial resources to achieve goals, AND...

. . . we also need a *Talent Review process* to identify top talent to achieve goals.

We need a *risk management* plan to mitigate or prevent business losses, AND...

...we also need *Succession Management* to mitigate or prevent talent losses.

We must continuously focus on *business development* to stay competitive, AND...

...we must also continuously focus on *Talent Development* to stay competitive.

Successful organizations not only focus diligently on reviewing and developing their *financial strength*—they also focus diligently on reviewing and developing their *talent benchstrength!*

What Does a Strong Talent Benchstrength Strategy Look Like?

It is easy to say that an organization strives to develop a strong talent benchstrength, but what does this really "look like" in the organization?

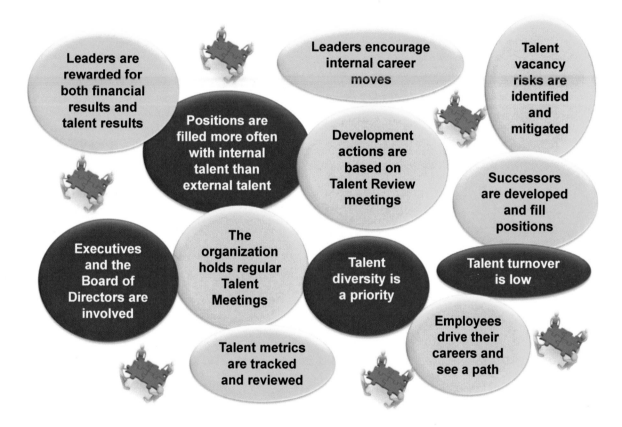

Notice that a strong Talent Benchstrength culture is a team effort, requiring the involvement of the Board of Directors, executives, business leaders and employees. Everyone in the organization will need to understand the Talent Benchstrength strategy, processes, resources and tools, and everyone will need to understand their role and responsibilities.

How Will a Strong Talent Benchstrength Save Time and Money?

Talent and succession management are business functions designed to save recruiting expenses, and to focus leadership development funds in ways that will retain and develop top talent.   Talent Benchstrength can save time and money in the following ways:

REDUCED RECRUITING EXPENSES: You will decrease your external recruiting costs and the costs of onboarding and training new talent.

RISK MANAGEMENT: Your retention of top talent increases and your organization becomes more aware of (and prepared for) talent loss risks.

READINESS: Talent will be more prepared for new business challenges and for new positions, resulting in faster and more successful internal career transitions.

NEW GROWTH: You will align the business goals and the growth of the organization with the identification and development of talent and competencies needed to achieve new goals.

DEVELOPMENT DOLLARS ARE WELL-SPENT: Leadership development is tied to future leadership talent needs, to employee career interests and to actual succession plans for specific competency growth.

ACCOUNTABILITY: Talent Benchstrength tools and processes increase development action follow-through, which increases the readiness of successor candidates.

REDUCED OPPORTUNITY LOSS: Your open position "time-to-fill" and interview time for talent vacancies will decrease, which also reduces lost business opportunities.

Why Do I Keep Hearing About Talent Issues?

There has been an increase in interest in talent benchstrength and succession planning in recent years. There are many reasons for the continuing growth of this business function:

A growing retirement population

Flat organization structures with fewer development steps

Expectations of emerging generations of talent

An increase in top employees starting their own businesses

Global population changes

An expanding need for top talent for innovation and leadership

The high cost of external recruiting and top talent turnover

As these talent forces continue to grow, so does the need for Talent Benchstrength!

Do We Still Need a Performance Management Strategy?

As a business leader you are already providing performance appraisals for employees, so you may be wondering why the company also needs talent benchstrength processes. You are correct that both of these processes are designed to increase employee engagement (motivational levels) and employee performance.

But, the major difference between Performance Management and a Talent Benchstrength Strategy is…

Performance Management measures PAST Individual Talent Performance

Talent Benchstrength focuses on FUTURE Talent Needs, Risks and Development Actions

Reviewing Past Performance and Predicting Future Resources

All successful organizations continuously review past performance and identify strategies and resources needed for the future.

To demonstrate this, the chart below compares financial and talent strategies and processes, to review how we look at our past performance and how we predict future resource needs:

	Processes and Tools: Reviewing Past Performance ⬅	Processes and Tools: Predicting Future Resources ➡
Financial Resources	Annual Report Profit and Loss Reports Balance Sheets Profit Margin Calculations	Budgeting Processes Financial Forecasting Sales Projections Inventory Processes
Talent Resources	Performance Appraisals Employee Recognition Mid-Year Review Discussions Merit Salary Increases and/or Bonuses	Talent Assessments Succession Planning and Development Talent Review Meetings Top Talent Identification and Development

Every organization has a vision of providing something of value to customers, and every organization needs capital and talent to make that vision happen every day.

Identify Talent Resources to Achieve Your Business Goals

When leaders develop their budgets each year, they identify and request the FINANCIAL RESOURCES they will need to achieve those goals.

Similarly, the Talent Benchstrength process enables leaders to identify the TALENT RESOURCES AND ACTIONS needed to achieve their goals. An example of this thought process is shown below:

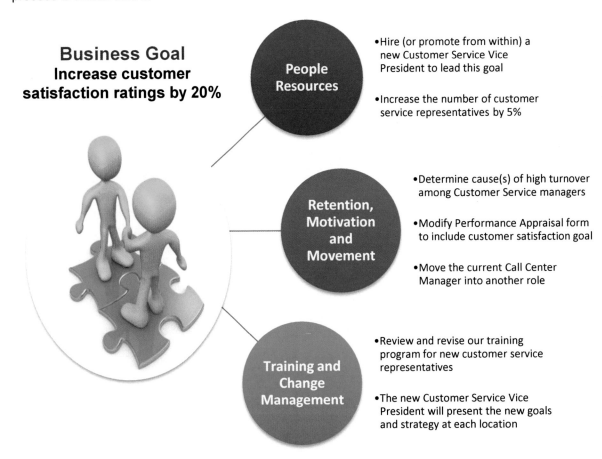

Business Goal
Increase customer satisfaction ratings by 20%

People Resources

- Hire (or promote from within) a new Customer Service Vice President to lead this goal
- Increase the number of customer service representatives by 5%

Retention, Motivation and Movement

- Determine cause(s) of high turnover among Customer Service managers
- Modify Performance Appraisal form to include customer satisfaction goal
- Move the current Call Center Manager into another role

Training and Change Management

- Review and revise our training program for new customer service representatives
- The new Customer Service Vice President will present the new goals and strategy at each location

Keep your Sales <u>and</u> Leadership Pipelines Full!

What does it really mean to have a strong leadership pipeline?

First, think of a successful sales group. The organization will have new customer markets they are just looking into, potential customers they are contacting for the first time, prospective customers who are in the sales process, customers who are about to make a purchase or close a deal, and current customers.

The Sales Pipeline

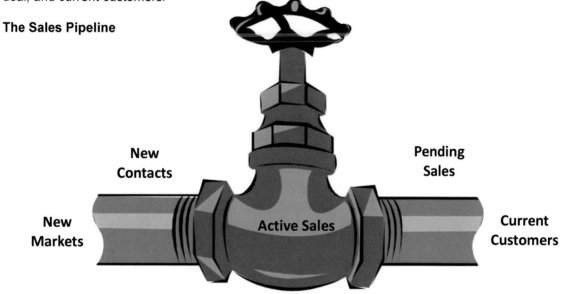

New Contacts

Pending Sales

New Markets

Active Sales

Current Customers

Consider what would occur if there were any gaps in the <u>SALES PIPELINE</u>:

- If new markets and new contacts are not pursued, current markets become saturated and the competition may gain a new market edge

- A decrease in new contacts, active and pending sales will weaken financial results

- If the organization loses current customers, there is an immediate impact to the company

If any part of the pipeline is weak, it will affect the company's financial position sooner or later. This is why every successful business leader reviews every aspect of their sales pipeline continuously to keep it full at each point in the sales process.

The Leadership Pipeline

Now apply these Sales Pipeline concepts to your <u>LEADERSHIP PIPELINE</u>:

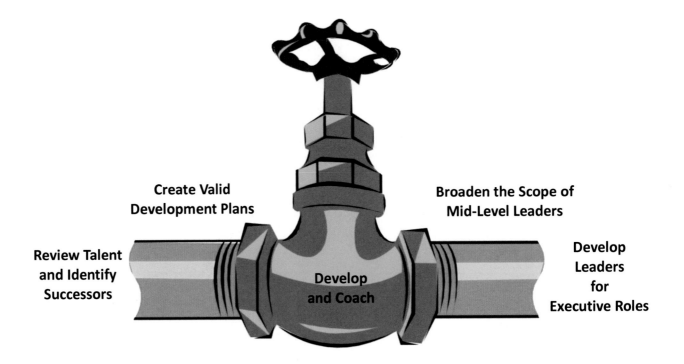

- Just as you continue to review and develop new markets for your products and services, it is important to review and develop your **internal new talent markets**, defined as your current employees who demonstrate the desire and ability to be your next front-line supervisors and mid-level managers

- Develop your current leaders to broaden their scope, strategic thinking, and people skills

- Continue to develop your senior leaders to develop a pool of prepared future executives

What Can We Learn From Sports Teams?

It is interesting to observe that coaches of sports teams focus virtually all of their time and energy on their team, **and that they are rewarded for and held accountable to team success**—not to their results as an individual. How can we apply this "culture of coaching" in our organizations?

The MOST important job of a sports coach is to <u>identify, retain and develop top talent</u>. On and off of the field, a sports coach spends most of his or her time coaching and developing players individually and with the team as a whole. Imagine a sports coach who spends most of his or her time doing paperwork in an office—how long would that coach have a job?

ALL sports coaches <u>identify and develop successors</u> as a top priority. In the sports world we refer to this talent as "the bench" and in the corporate world call this talent "successor candidates".   In the sports world, a coach who fails to identify and develop a strong bench will not keep their job very long.

To be successful, a sports coach must <u>align strengths with positions</u>, and give employees opportunities to leverage their strengths. Imagine a soccer coach putting a world-class goalie into a field-player position, or a football coach telling a quarterback to practice his kicking skills. Again, neither of these coaches would keep their job very long.

> *How do you prioritize your time and attention as a leader?*

The Succession Plan Analogy for Coffee Lovers

All around the world, people enjoy their coffee! The next time you enjoy that cup of coffee, think about the years it takes to grow coffee beans, and how the best coffee grows in the right environment, with the right amount of attention to the "needs" of the coffee plant, to ensure the plant has the right amount of fertilizer and water to thrive.

How can we apply these same concepts to the growth of top talent and successor candidates?

It takes 3-4 years for a coffee plant to produce coffee beans.	Planting a coffee seed and walking away will not produce coffee beans.	Watering a coffee plant once or twice a year will not produce coffee beans.
Similarly, it can take 3-4 years to develop a successor for a complex leadership role.	Similarly, putting a name on a successor chart and walking away will not produce Qualified Successors.	Similarly, sending a successor to a workshop once or twice a year will not produce a Qualified Successor.

Talent Benchstrength Functions

The functions of Talent Benchstrength and the organizational structure required will vary greatly based on the size, shape and maturity of each organization. You may need an entire Talent Benchstrength team to lead your talent strategy, or you may need a key Human Resources professional to work with business leaders to identify and develop successors and key talent.

Talent Benchstrength is an umbrella term that may include these functions:

- Leadership Development

- New Employee Orientation and Onboarding

- Career Movement and Internal Recruiting

- Job Rotational Assignments

- Succession Planning

- Performance Management

- Talent Assessment Tools and Processes

- Talent Review Meetings

- High Potential Employee Identification and Development

- Key Expert Employee Identification and Retention

- Identification of Critical Positions

- Identification and Development of Talent Pools

How Do I Identify Talent to Build Benchstrength?

When reviewing your team to identify high potentials and successors, consider their past performance, their future readiness, their qualifications for the position, and information from your discussions with employees about their own career interests.

Past Performance	Future Readiness	Employee Career Discussions
Previous Performance Review Results	Learning Agility and Strategic Thinking Ability	Does the employee's career interests align with the organizational needs?
Business Results - Key Accomplishments	Ability to deal with stress and work in an ambigous environment	Is the employee willing to take on new and challenging job roles?
Past Career Progression	Ability and desire to advance as a leader into more complex roles	Does the employee want to progress in a leadership development track?
Has learned from mistakes, is a continuous learner, and seeks feedback	Demonstrates superior people skills and respects others	Is the employee willing to take lateral career moves to build new skills?

Chapter Two
A Balanced Talent Strategy

Recruiting new talent outside of the company is an important part of your talent strategy, *but it should not be your entire talent strategy*.

It is important to balance an <u>internal</u> talent benchstrength strategy with an <u>external</u> recruiting strategy, by having internal talent benchstrength staff, budget, systems, and processes as well as external talent acquisition staff, budget, systems, and processes.

External recruiting focuses on sourcing, interviewing, evaluating, hiring and onboarding new talent from outside of the organization. This is an important part of the overall talent strategy in every organization to bring in fresh ideas and new skills into your organization.

But becoming dependent primarily on external sources for talent means that you are depending on your competitors to do a better job of developing their talent than you are…and that you are dependent on the assumption of a ready source of top talent even as economic conditions change.

Talent Acquisition
Fresh Ideas
New Competencies
Required for Growth

Talent Benchstrength
Retains Top Talent
Retains Knowledge
Builds Culture

The Business Dynamics of an Agile Talent Strategy

Organizations should make sure their talent strategy remains agile and appropriately balanced.

The Start-Up Organization:

The company has a small number of employees INSIDE of the company…	…so to grow the business, more employees must be hired from OUTSIDE of the company. There are simply not enough talent resources or competencies inside the company to support the business goals, to handle a wide variety of responsibilities, or to be ready to move into new positions.

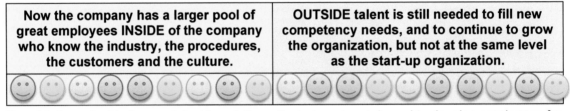

At this point, an **external** talent acquisition strategy makes good business sense, and at this stage it is normal to fill more positions with external talent than with internal talent career moves.

The Maturing-Growing Organization:

Now the company has a larger pool of great employees INSIDE of the company who know the industry, the procedures, the customers and the culture.	OUTSIDE talent is still needed to fill new competency needs, and to continue to grow the organization, but not at the same level as the start-up organization.

Now it is important to have a talent benchstrength strategy to retain and to develop employees for internal career growth, and to create a **balanced** internal and external talent strategy.

The Mature Organization:

Now the company has diligently selected top talent to create its competitive edge. The INTERNAL talent population now far exceeds the number of external new employees hired each year, and many of these employees want to grow within the company.	Now EXTERNAL talent should be needed far less frequently.

By this point, the company should focus the priority, the time and the budget on **internal** talent benchstrength, development actions and career growth, to avoid a talent acquisition dependency.

The Talent Acquisition Addiction Cycle

While a start-up company must rely on new external talent to grow, a "talent acquisition addiction" can form if the company continues to depend primarily on an external talent acquisition strategy.

Here is a scenario of an organization with an <u>unbalanced talent strategy</u>:

Internal Talent Benchstrength	External Talent Acquisition
Number of talented people in the organization…	New employees hired annually:
Budget for Internal Talent-Succession Strategy: $	Budget for Talent Acquisition: $$$$$
Talent Benchstrength / Succession Staff:	Talent Acquisition Staff:
Computer System for Internal Talent Tracking, Succession Plans, Development Actions? **No**	Computer System for Talent Acquisition? **Yes**
Budget for Leadership Development, Key Talent Retention Plans, Executive Coaching: $$	Budget for External Search Fees, Hiring Bonuses, Marketing: $$$$$$

So what is going on here from a business standpoint?

1. **The company is still using a "start-up" talent strategy** rather than shifting staff, time and budget to an internal talent benchstrength strategy to retain and develop top talent.

2. The company is spending the MOST money on the FEWEST people, *and it is spending the most money on the people who are relatively unknown assets to the company.*

3. Now top talent sees that the company does not invest in its people, and that the company rarely fills positions from within, so this top talent leaves the company.

4. Therefore, the company now has to spend even more money on external search fees, on hiring bonuses, and on higher salaries to try to replace top talent to remain competive.

If this cycle continues, the company becomes addicted to constantly replacing talent from the external talent market. The company is now dependent on the availability of "ready talent" in the marketplace, and like any addiction, this becomes a costly habit.

Talent Benchstrength Actions

The key actions involved in a Talent Benchstrength strategy include a consistent Talent Review Process, Succession Management, and Talent Development.

> The **Talent Review Process** is about *proactively* and *regularly* discussing, planning and acting on talent needs for ongoing employee and business performance and success.
>
> **Succession Management** is a business risk management function that just happens to be about people. Succession planning is designed to review talent vacancy risks and to form retention and development plans to reduce this risk.
>
> **Talent Development** provides the on-the-job experiences and formal training resources to enhance strengths, to build job qualifications and to address gaps.

All organizations should have external talent acquisition and internal talent benchstrength strategies, tools and processes. The focus of <u>internal</u> talent benchstrength pertains more to the retention and development of current employees, rather than just sourcing new talent externally. **Without a strong internal talent benchstrength, an organization is betting on having a ready supply of external talent to fill most positions as the company grows and as positions become vacant, which is both risky and costly.**

The knowledge and skill sets of employees in your <u>external</u> talent recruiting roles are very different from those who are responsible for internal Talent Benchstrength, as shown below:

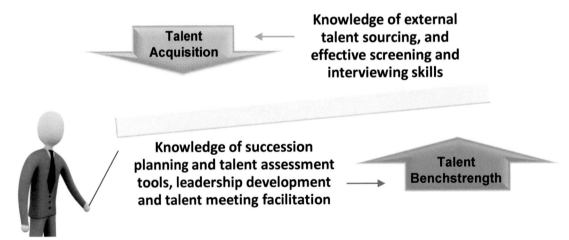

Talent Acquisition ← Knowledge of external talent sourcing, and effective screening and interviewing skills

Knowledge of succession planning and talent assessment tools, leadership development and talent meeting facilitation → Talent Benchstrength

What is My Role in Talent Benchstrength as a Leader?

As a leader in the organization, your role is critical to achieve the expected talent benchstrength business results. Leaders are expected to:

- Serve as a role model of these talent benchstrength processes

- Follow through with all expected talent development actions and deadlines

- Communicate talent benchstrength strategy and processes to employees

Typical business leader actions for each talent benchstrength function are shown below:

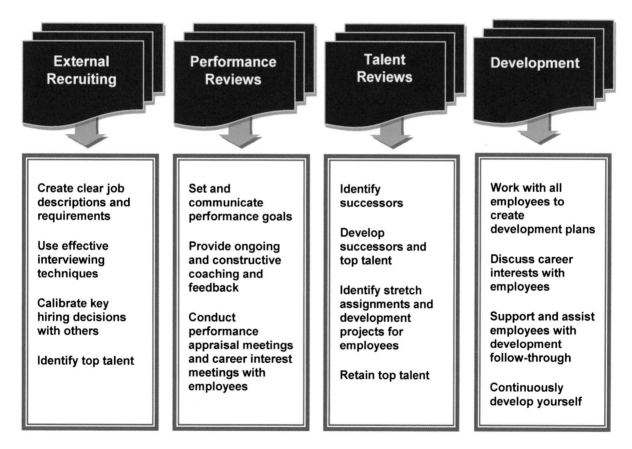

External Recruiting	Performance Reviews	Talent Reviews	Development
Create clear job descriptions and requirements Use effective interviewing techniques Calibrate key hiring decisions with others Identify top talent	Set and communicate performance goals Provide ongoing and constructive coaching and feedback Conduct performance appraisal meetings and career interest meetings with employees	Identify successors Develop successors and top talent Identify stretch assignments and development projects for employees Retain top talent	Work with all employees to create development plans Discuss career interests with employees Support and assist employees with development follow-through Continuously develop yourself

Talent Benchstrength: A Win-Win for Everyone

 Talent benchstrength and succession planning processes are business tools that are designed to analyze data, to make informed decisions, and to reduce risk (leadership vacancy risk). **A Talent Benchstrength strategy is critical for the company and it is also important to employees, as shown below:**

Advantages to Employees	Advantages to the Business
The process enables employees to communicate career interests, past work experience and competencies to managers on a regular basis.	Just as leaders assess other business risks and form contingency plans, they are now assessing and forming contingency plans for talent vacancy risk.
Employees know that leaders are discussing potential career paths and ideas for their development.	The process provides a forum, a timeslot and a structure to discuss talent and performance as a leadership team.
The employee's development actions will be designed to leverage their strengths and to develop competencies that lead to potential career growth in the organization.	The process serves as a "talent inventory" that increases the visibility of top talent, identifies positions with missing successors, and plans for the future talent needs of the organization.
Employees see that a long-term career exists for them at the company with growth and opportunity.	The costs involved in hiring and onboarding external candidates for vacant positions begin to decrease, and the dependency on the external talent market decreases.

Integrate Talent Benchstrength Into Your Business Calendar

Elevate talent benchstrength goals and actions to the same level of importance as all other business requirements in your organization, and ensure these actions are seen as business requirements and not as separate or sidebar "HR activities". For example...

- Integrate talent organizational strengths and results into your Annual Report.

- Integrate succession plan updates and talent development progress discussions into your regular business strategy meetings, and into meetings with your Board of Directors.

- Integrate talent benchstrength metrics into your corporate balanced scorecard.

- Integrate talent benchstrength requirements into the leadership compensation or bonus structure to increase rewards and accountability.

Integrate talent benchstrength actions into your annual business calendar of events. Establish a talent benchstrength annual schedule as shown in the example below:

1st Quarter
- Goal Setting
- Merit / Bonus Awards
- Development Progress Meetings

2nd Quarter
- Succession Planning and Talent Review Meetings

3rd Quarter
- Update Development Plans
- Workforce Planning

4th Quarter
- Career Discussions
- Performance Reviews

A lack of succession planning for leaders and key experts is like coaching a soccer team with only first-string players— everything is great until you lose a key player with no one on the bench ready to play, leaving a gaping hole and an advantage for the competitor.

Doris Sims Spies, SPHR

Chapter Three

Talent Concepts and Definitions

High Performers, High Potentials, and Successors…could we have some clarification please?

In this chapter, we will review talent benchstrength and talent concepts in more detail. We'll look at definitions of successors, high performers, high potentials, key experts, talent pools, and critical positions.

High Performers and High Potentials

A "Point-In-Time" Designation…

While every employee is expected to be a *high performing* employee throughout his or her career, the designation of being a *high potential* employee should be considered a "point-in-time" status.

Everyone is expected to be a HIGH PERFORMER **throughout their career, and the goal of every organization is to hire, retain and develop high performers.**

High Performers may also be HIGH POTENTIALS **at one or more specific points of time in their career, when they are ready and able to take on:**

- Challenging career assignments and projects with high visibility
- Additional development actions, coaching and feedback
- A larger scope of leadership responsibility
- Cross-functional lateral career moves (to build a wide breadth of knowledge and skills) in addition to promotional career moves
- A relocation job assignment as needed for organizational growth and change

---

It is also important to communicate to everyone that being identified as a high potential is not a "stamp on the forehead for life"; it is a **point-in-time development strategy**.   Employees will move in and move out of the high potential population or program over time. In other words, the company is saying to the employee, "At this point in your career we see that you are demonstrating exceptional ability and the desire for focused development, challenging job assignments and potential leadership career growth".

You may also want to define high potential employees at different levels in the organization and provide the most appropriate development for these groups; for example, you might have a group of "emerging high potentials" and a group of "executive potentials".

What is a High Potential?

The term "High Potential" is used to identify people who demonstrate top ASPIRATIONS and top ABILITIES <u>at the same time</u>. The traits below define characteristics of superior aspirations and abilities. While everyone demonstrates strengths and development areas, if an individual demonstrates a significant weakness in of any of these traits (or if the individual violates one of the traits) these issues should be addressed *before* identifying the person as a High Potential.

Aspirations	Abilities
Desires leadership advancement into more complex roles	Demonstrates the business acumen to move into significant leadership roles
Is open to career movement into challenging new roles and/or relocation	Demonstrates innovation, strategic thinking skills and creativity
Is willing to move laterally to increase breadth of skills	Demonstrates learning agility to succeed in a rapidly changing environment
Seeks and acts on feedback for continuous improvement	Demonstrates superior interpersonal skills and is respected by others
Follows through with learning assignments and development actions	Effectively deals with stress, organizational politics and emotions
Is self-motivated and highly engaged in the organization	Leverages strengths and develops (or compensates for) weaknesses

What is a Successor?

The Succession Planning process typically identifies:

- Successors for specific replacement positions
- Talent pools for positions with similar competencies
- Qualification gaps that must be fulfilled or corrected to develop Future Successors into Qualified Successor candidates

You will need to form definitions for leaders to identify successors in a consistent fashion. Some sample definitions are shown below.

Successor Definitions

Qualified Successors: Employees who currently possess and demonstrate all of the required qualifications for the incumbent's position.

This does not mean that a Qualified Successor for the position has *every* competency that the incumbent leader demonstrates, but they are qualified to interview for the position, and they are qualified to be considered for the position if it were vacant today. They are at least as qualified as an external candidate that the company would consider for this position, if not more so.

To identify Qualified Successors, ask the question, "If the position were open today, which employees in the company would be qualified to interview for the position now?"

Future-Gap Successors: Employees who are not currently qualified for the incumbent's position but who demonstrate the abilities and the aspirations to develop the competencies, education, and/or work experience within a short timeframe. Identifying competency gaps also leads into specific development action planning for successors, as shown in this example:

Abby is a Future 2-Gap Successor for the HR Director role. To become a Qualified Successor, she would need to 1) obtain her Senior Professional in Human Resources (SPHR) certification, and 2) obtain experience and confidence working with Director-level leaders. Abby's development plan will include the requirements to obtain the SPHR certification by a specific date, and to work on a Director-level project team by a specific date to begin to work with Director-level leaders.

Emergency Candidates: One or more employees who could handle the position on a temporary basis until the incumbent returns from a leave of absence or until the position is filled. Often the emergency candidates will take on expanded job responsibilities of the incumbent until the position is filled.

What is a Key Expert?

In addition to identifying high potentials and successors, some organizations also identify employees who are key experts. In some organizations, key expert employees are more critical (and/or are would be more difficult to replace) than the top executives of the organization.

Key Experts have achieved a distinguished level of expertise in their field. Key experts contribute in significant and unique ways in the company, but they may not have the desire or the ability to move quickly into new leadership roles, and they are often not interested in lateral career moves.

The unique competency set of a key expert (which should include extensive knowledge and experience within the company as well as specialized skill sets and qualifications) would be nearly impossible to replace if the individual left the organization. For this reason, key experts should identify and develop their own successors just as leaders do, and they should provide training and serve in mentor roles to others within the organization.

The primary purpose of a Key Expert program is to RECOGNIZE and RETAIN employees who prefer to pursue a career track of significant expertise rather than focusing on significant advancement in a leadership track.

Many key experts also serve on external boards and committees that influence their industry, and they may publish papers, create new patents for the company, and serve as speakers to provide more positive visibility and publicity for their company.

Organizations that identify key experts typically provide stock options or other compensation retention packages to these individuals. Organizations with a key expert identification strategy typically have a significant population of employees who are highly educated, qualified and specialized in their field.

What is a Talent Pool?

Identifying a Talent Pool is a process used to select:

- Multiple successor candidates for specific replacement positions

- Top Talent groups for positions with similar competencies

Creating talent pools is an effective way to develop talent for key positions. For example, if an organization has 50 Site Managers, rather than identifying individual successors for each Site Manager position, the organization can identify a talent pool of candidates who share the abilities and desire to move into this role in the future.

As successors and candidates for talent pools are identified, we also identify the qualification gaps that must be fulfilled or corrected to develop and prepare these individuals for future roles in the organization. Some successors are already qualified for the position, and others require additional knowledge, skills, experiences, and/or qualifications to be ready to move into the incumbent's position.

A talent pool describes a group of successor candidates who share the same abilities and aspirations to move into a specific role. For example, rather than creating ten <u>individual</u> successor plans for ten General Manager positions in a company, it makes sense to identify and to develop a General Manager <u>talent pool</u> of multiple successor candidates for this role. The talent pool candidates can then participate in a General Manager training program to increase their readiness for this position in the future.

What is a Critical Position?

An organization may decide to identify the most critical positions in order to:

- Place top talent in the most critical roles
- Focus succession planning efforts on the most critical roles
- Factor this information into the compensation structure for the role
- Identify roles that can't be eliminated due to regulartory requirements, safety issues, etc.
- Identify special skill set needs that are key to organizational success

It is important to understand that identifying critical roles has nothing to do with the individuals who are currently occupying those roles. Identifying critical <u>employees</u> (i.e. for retention purposes) is different from the exercise of identifying critical <u>positions</u>.

A simple assessment tool or spreadsheet can be created and used by business leaders to help identify critical roles. **Critical roles could have some or all of the following characteristics:**

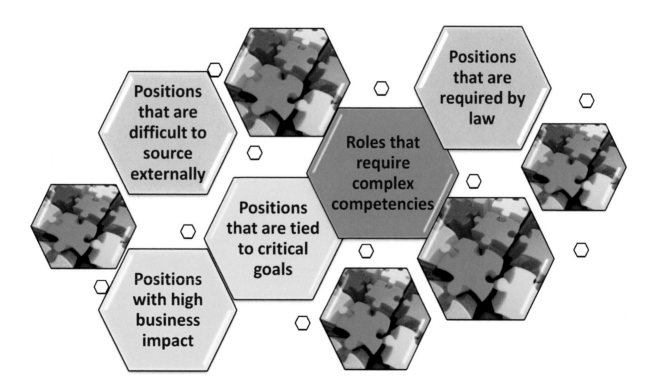

What is a Talent Review Meeting?

While performance management takes a look at the employee's past performance, behaviors and development actions, the Talent Review process is desigend to identify **future** talent and competency needs for the organization, and the future career interests of the employees.

During a Talent Review meeting, leaders discuss and agree on action plans for:

- Business goals and the corresponding talent and workforce planning needs

- Succession planning

- Identifying top talent and future business growth and leadership needs

- Reviewing potential vacancy risks and retention plans for top talent and successors

- Identifying positions without successors that may require external talent sourcing

- Identifying development actions to help prepare successors for future positions

Talent Review meetings are the central component of an effective talent benchstrength strategy. Leaders come together to discuss and to "fit the pieces together" to align business goals with the talent needs and with the career interests of employees.

A Talent Review Meeting is like a Budget Meeting or a Strategy Meeting, where the leaders discuss and calibrate business decisions together—the only difference is that the Talent Review meeting pertains to business decisions about the people in the organization.

What are Core Components of a Talent Benchstrength Strategy?

The Talent Review meeting is the center core of a strong Talent Benchstrength strategy. This is where leaders review talent, calibrate decisions about talent vacancy risk, identify top talent and successors, and agree on career and development action plans for employees.

The other components surrounding the central Talent Review meeting might vary in priority in different organizations, based on the business goals and "talent pain points". For example, an organization with a large percentage of potential retirements in the executive team should focus on succession planning and successor development as an urgent priority, while an organization that is growing and opening multiple new business locations should focus on identifying and developing a talent pool of leaders to lead in the new business locations. **There are no required components of a Talent Benchstrength strategy.**

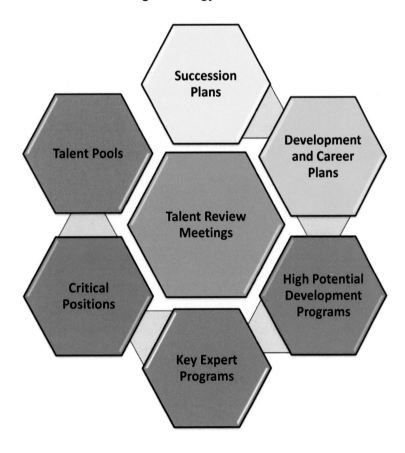

Succession Strategy vs. High Potential Strategy

While both a succession strategy and a high potential strategy are designed to increase leadership talent benchstrength, these strategies also serve different purposes, as shown below:

Succession Strategy

- Talent Vacancy Risk Management for Leaders and Key Experts

- Competency Development

- Replacement Planning

- Talent Pool Identification and Development

- Knowledge Retention

- Emergency Plans for Unexpected Leadership Absences / Departures

High Potential Strategy

- Leadership Growth Plans

- Talent Visibility

- Top Talent Identification, Retention and Development

- Leadership Development

- Leadership Career Movement and Job Assignments

- Preparation for New Leadership Expansion

What is a Talent Benchstrength (9-Box) Guide?

The Talent Benchstrength Guide is a **visual aid** to be used in Talent Review meetings to discuss the "point-in-time" in each person's career, and to identify appropriate development actions.

Talent Benchstrength® Guide

Successor and Top Talent Candidates

KE	**RE**	**UR**
<u>Key Expert</u> – These are "go-to" employees who mentor and provide expertise in the organization. Create a retention plan and a succession plan. Recognize their contributions, document their knowledge and ensure they train and mentor other employees.	<u>Ready Talent</u> –These employees demonstrate expert-level abilities and are ready for a lateral or promotional move if the opportunity presents itself in the organization. Identify career path options, a stretch assignment, a job rotation, opportunities for visibility, etc.	<u>Urgently Ready</u> – These employees demonstrate expertise-level abilities <u>and</u> superior leadership abilities, <u>and</u> they are urgently ready for a new challenge. Provide a senior mentor, and identify a new role or challenge. Provide accelerated leadership development, retention actions and recognition.
SA	**VT**	**ET**
<u>Solid Abilities</u> – These employees get the job done. They are loyal to the organization and are happy in their role. Recognize contributions and provide development to keep knowledge current. Leaders in this group should focus on coaching and developing others.	<u>Valued Talent</u> – These are solid ability employees who are actively gaining competencies and are highly engaged in their role. They express long-term career growth aspirations and are continuous learners. Provide coaching, career path ideas, development and recognition.	<u>Emerging Talent</u> – These employees demonstrate a strong desire for career growth, but they still have more competencies to develop to be ready for career growth. Discuss career path ideas, relocation aspirations, and development needs. Create a career path development plan that will enable this individual to develop new competencies.
AI	**UD**	**JF**
<u>Ability / Aspiration Issues</u> – Both Ability and Aspiration are below organizational expectations. Provide immediate feedback, coaching and a Performance Improvement Plan with scheduled coaching and progress meetings.	<u>Urgent Development</u> – Identify and act on development needs urgently to improve abilities and competencies. Identify career aspirations to increase motivation to perform. Provide frequent feedback and development resources, and recognize progress.	<u>Job Fit Issue</u> – Urgently provide a coaching session to listen, to provide feedback and to identify potential issues with job fit, employee engagement, performance, frustrations, etc. Identify why abilities are low and aspirations are high. Provide an action plan and monitor progress.

Ability (vertical axis): Low — Solid — High

Successor and Top Talent Candidates (right side vertical label)

Aspiration (horizontal axis): Low — •• Solid — High

Using the Talent Benchstrength Guide

Employees will move around on the Talent Benchstrength Guide at various points in their careers, based on fluctuating levels of ability and aspiration everyone experiences throughout their career. Most people (if not everyone) experiences "ability highs and lows" in our career (i.e. when we start in a new position) and "aspiration highs and lows" in our career (i.e. when we have a new priority in our lives or when we are not sure about our next career move).

Here are some ideas to consider when using the Guide:

NEW TALENT: Employees who have less than six months in their current role should not be placed on the Talent Benchstrength Guide because we don't have enough data in the new role to evaluate ability and aspiration for the next role. For these employees, ensure they have a new employee development plan or a transitional learning plan.

1SUCCESSOR CANDIDATES: The future leaders in the organization are primarily found within the blue and green boxes. Successor candidates should be selected from the blue and green boxes in the Guide.

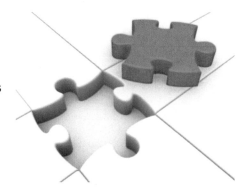

TALENT GROWTH AND DEVELOPMENT: Employees are <u>expected to move</u> within the blue and green boxes on the Talent Benchstrength Guide during their careers, in order to broaden their skillset and their mindset. A lack of employee movement within these boxes over multiple years is an indicator of a lack of business growth, and/or stagnant career growth for employees.

SOLID PERFORMERS AND KEY EXPERTS: Ultimately, most employees reach a Solid Abilities or a Key Expert level in their careers, as they reach their expertise peak and/or their own career aspiration peak. Employees in the purple boxes on the Guide provide critical knowledge, skills, and loyalty in the organization. These employees get the job done, and they can mentor others.

HIGH POTENTIALS: High Potentials should be selected from the green boxes on the Guide. The designation of "High Potential" identifies a point-in-time in an employee's career in which the individual is performing at peak ability, the individual demonstrates superior leadership skills, and the individual demonstrates high career aspirations and a strong need for learning and growth. Top talent will likely move into the High Potential "box" multiple times throughout their career, as they master new roles and are ready for more complex roles.

LOW ABILITIES OR ASPIRATIONS: Any employees who are designated in the tan/brown boxes on the Guide should receive immediate feedback, coaching, development plans and/or performance improvement plans to identify and address the issues. The maximum amount of time an employee might remain in a low performing box should be approximately one year.

Chapter Four
Succession Management

Succession management is the process of **proactively** identifying internal employees who are either fully qualified or nearly qualified to interview for positions in the organization if the position becomes vacant.   During the succession planning process, leaders also identify specific development actions that will increase successor candidate readiness for future roles.

Effective succession planning is designed to answer these questions:

The Goals of Succession Management

While there are no required talent benchstrength components, succession planning is a good business practice for any size, shape or type of organization. Succession planning protects the company and creates internal career path options and development actions for employees.

Succession Management is designed to:

- Be proactive and to be prepared for talent loss

- Be a critical risk management function

- Identify actions to develop competencies in successor candidates

- Identify potential talent losses without internal successor candidates which will require talent acquisition budget and actions

- Reduce the costs of external talent acquisition

- Retain top talent through career growth and development

- Demonstrate to long-term clients, to investors and to the Board of Directors that active plans are in place to protect the company from talent loss and to develop future leaders

Succession Management: A Risk Management Function

Every day our leaders use processes and tools to help make the best decisions possible—running a business successfully is both an art and a science. No "perfect" business tools and decision-making processes exist, but these tools help leaders make more informed decisions. In addition, business tools and processes are designed to reduce risk.

Examples of these processes and tools are shown in the box below. All of these processes are used to 1) analyze data, 2) reduce risks and 3) make informed decisions.

Mergers and Acquisitions: <u>Due Diligence</u>

New Product Expansion: <u>Market Analysis and Customer Feedback</u>

Advertising: <u>Focus Group Feedback</u>

Hiring New Employees: <u>The Interview Process</u>

Developing New Technology: <u>User Requirements Analysis</u>

Developing and Promoting New Leaders: <u>Talent Benchstrength</u>

Talent development and succession planning processes are business tools that are also designed to 1) analyze talent data, 2) make informed decisions to identify, retain and develop future leaders, and 3) reduce risk (talent vacancy risk).

The goal of talent and succession management is not to fill **all** positions internally; it is also important to bring in new talent with new ideas, perspectives and competencies. But as we work to develop internal talent, we will also increase retention of our top talent, our talent vacancy risks decrease, and our external recruiting costs decrease.

 **Succession Planning is a <u>risk management business</u> function designed to both prevent and to prepare for talent loss. It is a critical component of an organization's Talent Benchstrength strategy.**

How Do I Identify My Potential Successors?

Leaders at all levels in the organization should identify and develop successors to ensure business continuation and growth. But what criteria and process should leaders use to select potential successors? Here are some potential questions to consider when identifying successors:

- Is the candidate interested in my position?

- Does the candidate demonstrate both the desire and ability to be a leader, or are their talents better suited for an individual contributor role in the organization?

- Does the candidate demonstrate the strategic thinking skills required to keep the group or function moving forward?

- Is the candidate respected by others in the organization?

- Does the candidate possess the required educational requirements for the position?

To begin selecting potential successors, a leader can create a simple Competency Chart to identify the knowledge, skills and abilities required for their own position . . .

Knowledge	Skills	Abilities
BS Degree in Finance or Accounting	**People leadership skills – effective hiring, coaching and development of people**	**Has the ability to analyze financial data and form strategic plans from the data**
CPA – Certified Public Accountant designation	**Superior Excel spreadsheet skills and overall computer skills**	**Is able to influence cross-functionally and is respected by others**
Knowledge of budgeting strategies, tools and processes	**Demonstrates effective presentation skills to communicate financial plans**	**Is detail-oriented to ensure accuracy, but is also able to see the bigger picture**

. . . and then place the initials of potential successors on the chart if they already demonstrate the knowledge, skill and ability. This exercise will identify the most prepared successors, as well as identifying strengths and qualification gaps for each candidate. This is a <u>very simple way</u> to help identify valid successor candidates. If a current job description is available, use this to quickly build a simple competency chart.

Development Actions for Successor Candidates

The chart below is a very simple way to identify Qualified Successor candidates and Future Successor candidates and to identify development plans to increase candidate readiness.

Identifying successors as "Ready 1-2 Years" is often insufficient to develop successor candidates for positions. What companies often find is that year after year goes by, and the successor candidate is still "Ready 1-2 Years". This is because simply looking at **readiness timeframes** does not identify **qualification gaps or development actions** for the position. Identifying these gaps and development plans is the key to developing successor candidate readiness.

In the example below, we can see that KJ (Kathy Joe) has all of the qualifications for the role with the exception of people leadership skills and budgeting skills. So KJ is a Future 2-Gap Successor, and now we can identify specific development actions to address those gaps. Six months from now, we can also check on the progress of these very specific development actions.

Knowledge	Skills	Attributes / Talents
BS Degree in Finance or Accounting **GH, KJ, TM, LT, BM**	People leadership skills – effective hiring, coaching and development of people **TM, LT, BM**	Has the ability to analyze financial data and form strategic plans from the data **GH, KJ**
CPA – Certified Public Accountant designation **GH, KJ, TM, LT**	Superior Excel spreadsheet skills and overall computer skills **GH, KJ, TM, LT**	Is able to influence cross-functionally and is respected by others **KJ, TM**
Knowledge of budgeting strategies, tools and processes **LT, BM**	Demonstrates effective presentation skills to communicate financial plans **GH, KJ, TM**	Is detail-oriented to ensure accuracy, but is also able to see the bigger picture **GH, KJ, TM, LT**

KJ needs to develop leadership and budget skills before becoming a Qualified Successor, so she is a 2-Gap Successor Candidate. Development actions this year include:
1) **Participating in the budget process,**
2) **Attending management training and serving in a formal or informal manager role.**

Are All Successors Also High Potentials?

No—while all successor candidates should be high <u>performing</u> employees, many successors will not be identified as high <u>potential</u> employees. A successor may be an excellent candidate for a specific position in the organization, but may not currently have the desire or ability to advance and/or move laterally into multiple positions cross-functionally, as outlined below:

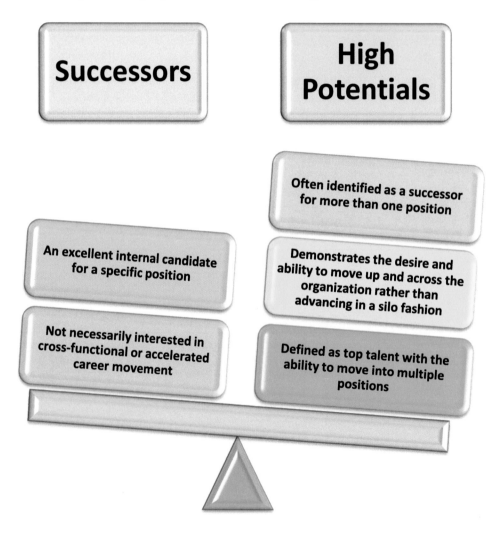

Successors

High Potentials

Often identified as a successor for more than one position

An excellent internal candidate for a specific position

Demonstrates the desire and ability to move up and across the organization rather than advancing in a silo fashion

Not necessarily interested in cross-functional or accelerated career movement

Defined as top talent with the ability to move into multiple positions

Should All High Potentials be Successors?

Typically yes—you will want to identify one or more successor roles for your high potential employees to move into, in order to place your key talent in the most critical positions in the company and to plan for the career growth of your top talent.

And consider this—if you have high potential employees who are not also Qualified Successors or Future-Gap Successors <u>somewhere</u> in the organization it begs the question…what do they have the potential to do in our organization?

Exceptions to this guideline would be high potentials who are placed in rotation positions to determine their strongest career path, and high potentials who are being groomed for positions that may not even exist yet in the organization.

Will we have more successors or more high potential employees in our organization?

You will have more successor candidates than high potentials, because you will want to identify at least one successor candidate for each leader. So you may have hundreds or thousands of successor candidates.

However, most organizations identify 5% or less of the organization for the high potential talent group. Therefore, this group is typically much smaller than the group of successor candidates.

Identify Your Future Leadership Talent Needs

Another important succession management strategic planning process for leaders is to take a look at the future leadership position needs that are expected for the future year and beyond.

To determine future leadership talent needs, consider:

New Goals

- Do I need new leaders to achieve new goals?

- Do I need to expand the roles of current leaders?

- Do my current leaders have the skill sets and attributes needed to achieve our current and future goals?

Growth

- What is the ratio of leaders to employees - is this ratio appropriate?

- Do I need more (or fewer) leaders in the coming year(s) to lead our employees?

- Are we opening sites or stores in new locations which will require new leaders?

Vacancies

- Do I have leaders who have expressed retirement plans and/or will be eligible to retire?

- Do I have leaders with a high vacancy risk of leaving my group or the organization who may need to be replaced?

- Do I currently have open leadership positions to be filled?

Chapter Five
Talent Review Meetings

The Talent Benchstrength process can be defined in three distinct Talent Review phases:

1. **Preparation:** Before leaders attend a Talent Review meeting, they should:

    - **Talk with employees about their career interests, relocation ability (if applicable) and development needs**

    - **Put together a draft succession plan for their own position**

    - **Assess employee performance, leadership ability, and aspirations**

2. **Talent Review Meetings:** Business leaders meet together to discuss talent resources and needs and to agree on the identification of top talent and successors.

3. **Follow Up and Development Actions:** Leaders and employees follow through with the development plans and other actions identified in the Talent Meeting.

Talent Profile Updates

Talent Assessments

Talent Review Meetings

Analysis/Recommendations

Development Plans

The Preparation Phase: What is Talent Assessment?

Talent Assessment enables both leaders and employees to gather information prior to the Talent Review meetings about leadership and career growth abilities and interests. It is similar to the work that leaders do before going into a budget meeting—no leader would ever consider going into a budget discussion session without preparing budget projections, run-rate figures, vendor quotes, justifications, etc.

Similarly, leaders should never consider going into a Talent Review meeting without reviewing past performance appraisals, and discussing career, relocation and development interests with employees. Prior to the Talent Review meeting, leaders should also rate the future leadership potential of every employee who will be reviewed in the meeting.

A best practice Talent Assessment process should include three key components:

A Review of **Past Performance**

An Assessment of **Future Potential**

Career Discussions with Employees

Consistency in your talent assessment methodology is critical to create a fair and legally defensible internal talent identification process. The high potential and successor identification criteria and talent assessment process must be duplicated identically across the organization or the groups that are assessed, to ensure all talent is evaluated in the same way.

The Calibration Phase: Talent Review Discussions

The Talent Review Meeting is a STRUCTURED and FACILITATED session designed for the discussion of current and future leadership talent in the organization. The meeting is attended by business leaders and is typically facilitated by a Human Resource professional.

The Talent Review Meeting…

…increases the VISIBILITY of talent in the organization.

…increases the VALIDITY of the succession plans and high potential employee selections.

The Talent Review meeting gathers data regarding the observations and perspectives of multiple leaders in the company, rather than basing Talent Benchstrength decisions on a single manager's perspective or on a single rating system.

The agenda for the Talent Review Meeting will vary based on the organization's business goals, size and culture, but some examples of agenda topics include:

Data to review and discuss…

- **Business Goals and Talent Needs**
- **Individual Talent Profiles and 9-Box Discussions**
- **Vacancy Risk and Impact Assessment**
- **Strengths and Development Needs of Individuals**

Decisions to make…

- **Successor Candidate Identification**
- **Talent Mobility and Potential Career Paths**
- **Development Action Plans**
- **Agreement of High Potentials and Talent Pools**

What is My Role in the Talent Review Meeting?

Just as you would prepare financial spreadsheets and justifications before attending a budget meeting, you should prepare data and documents for your Talent Review meeting:

Before the Meeting

- Create your own succession plan and identify your high potential employees; discuss this with your own manager

- Obtain a Talent Profile (or a current resume) from each employee

- Talk with employees about career path ideas, relocation ability, and interest in advancing as a leader

- Complete a talent assessment process, and/or review past Performance Appraisals of employees

During the Meeting

- Bring your employees' Talent Profiles and career interest notes to the meeting

- Be objective; use factual business data points when discussing talent and succession plans

- It is important to listen to all discussions; employees from other groups may be your next top talent

- Keep the "big picture" in mind - encourage cross-functional employee career movement

After the Meeting

- Discuss development plan actions from the Talent Review meeting with employees as appropriate

- Work with employees to follow through on Talent Review meeting action plans throughout the year

- Work with Human Resources to update succession plans as needed during the year

- Use the succession plans and internal talent information to fill newly vacant positions

Notifying and Developing High Potentials

When organizations identify high potential employees, they must determine how they will communicate and execute their strategy to develop these employees.

Will you notify your high potential employees and provide a special development program for these individuals?

When determining your notification strategy, consider that you have multiple notification options:

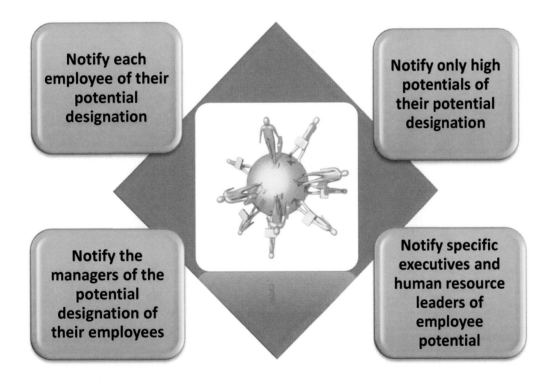

Each of these notification strategies has merit—**the only notification strategy to avoid is to not communicate a clear notification strategy at all, resulting in an informal process in which some leaders notify high potential employees and others do not.** This will result in an inconsistent process that could be perceived as biased and even discriminatory by employees.

High Potential Notification: Advantages and Disadvantages

The decision to notify high potential employees continues to be a very controversial one, and at this time no clear best practice has emerged pertaining to this decision.

Companies can use the following chart to help make this decision—consider the goals of your Talent Benchstrength strategy and the culture of your organization when determining your notification plan:

Advantages of Choosing to Notify High Potentials	Advantages of Choosing Not to Notify High Potentials
Results in a higher retention rate of High Potentials	Reduces concern regarding morale issues of employees not currently identified as High Potentials
Increases the ability to provide development resources and programs to High Potentials	Promotes an environment that all employees are expected to be high performers
Increases the ability to measure the results of the High Potential Program	Reduces concern about the need to move employees out of the High Potential program in the future
Results in a greater transparency pertaining to career development to motivate employees	Eliminates the cost and time required to provide focused development opportunities for High Potentials
Increases the ability to create and execute cross-functional career moves for High Potentials	Emphasizes the development strategy that each manager is responsible for providing on-the-job development

Chapter Six
Talent Development

Out with the Career Ladder—In With the Career Lattice. . .

The old perception of advancing up the "career ladder" is no longer applicable in today's work environment, where moving only in a silo fashion "up the ladder" doesn't serve either employees or the company.

For employees, this type of career plan provides very limited career opportunities, and the employee risks being "typecast" into one career option.

For the company, this type of career plan provides very limited internal candidates for open and new growth positions, and creates employees with knowledge, skills and abilities that are limited to one functional area.

The Career Lattice

Using the concept of a CAREER LATTICE, career growth should include <u>BOTH</u>:

- *Multiple lateral moves* into new functional areas, to develop a wide breadth of competencies, to build relationships across the organization, and to increase the ability to "see the bigger picture"

- *Advancement career moves* into positions with higher levels of responsibility, visibility and complexity, to build leadership skills, organizational savvy traits, and higher-level strategic thinking skills

Using a career lattice model for development provides employees with a variety of job experiences designed to increase knowledge depth and a broad skill set. A good developmental career opportunity meets the company's business needs while also meeting the career interests and developmental needs of the employee.

Follow-Up—How Does Human Resources Support You?

The follow-up actions and development that occur after the Talent Review meeting are a critical part of the Talent Benchstrength process—this is "where the rubber meets the road."

After the Talent Review Meeting...

...Human Resources and Business Leaders analyze the talent data to identify trends, themes and additional action plans.

...Human Resources and Business Leaders may create Talent Reports and/or presentations to communicate results and recommendations.

...Employees create or update their Individual Development Plans and follow-through with their development actions.

...Human Resources and Business Leaders actively develop Successors and High Potential Employees throughout the year.

...Human Resources and Business Leaders execute actions as discussed and documented in Talent Review meetings. Progress meetings are recommended mid-year to review development action progress.

Leadership Development Tools and Resources

The following chart is an example of the tools and resources an organization might provide to assist leaders in the development planning process, and to address specific competency needs:

What is it?	Why do we need this?	Target Group
High Potential Leadership Program	**This 2-year program is designed to accelerate the leadership skills, mindset and career movement of those who are identified as high potential leaders.**	**High Potentials as identified in Talent Review meetings**
On-the-Job Development Guide	**To provide development suggestions (such as activities, reading, training) to support an individual's growth and to build leadership competencies.**	**All employees**
IDP: Individual Development Plans	**To identify and document specific development actions for individual employees. IDPs should be created or updated at least annually, following Talent Review meetings.**	**All employees**
Onboarding Plans	**To identify onboarding and training needs to accelerate the transition of new employees**	**New employees**
Individual Assessments and Coaching: **360 Feedback Assessments**	**To provide feedback and to increase self-awareness to form a development plan. Each leader should complete a 360 feedback process every year.**	**All leaders**
Leadership Foundational Program	**To provide management training for leaders who are newly promoted and for new employees entering the organization in a management position, regardless of position.**	**New managers**

Sample High Potential Development Program

Leadership development programs should include activities that align with the organizational leadership competencies to build these leadership skills and to build the company culture. Additionally, the program should be individualized to leverage a person's strengths while also addressing competency gaps and career growth actions.

Core Elements are activities that everyone in the program completes together, while the additional development actions would be customized to each participant. **Ideally, the High Potential program includes both structured learning and on-the-job development.**

Core Elements	Leading for Growth Conference	360 Feedback and Talent Development Workshop	Executive Sponsor – meet at least quarterly	Interview with Recruiting Leader of Leadership Talent

Note: All participants must complete the Foundations of Leadership program for their management level, if not completely previously.

Leadership Essentials	Ideas for: On-the-Job Development	Facilitator-Led Workshops	Self-Study Options B-Books, C-CD ROM and/or E-Learning
Getting Results	Referring to the Corporate Scorecard, identify a new metric for one of your job responsibilities to demonstrate increased profitability, enhanced delivery to customers, increased value, and/or enhanced associated engagement.	Process Reality Crucial Conversations Leading for Growth The OZ Principle of Accountability	B-The OZ Principle of Accountability: Hickman E-Why Finance Matters Course
Interpersonal Skills	Work with your HR Partner or a 360 coach to identify and form a plan to improve a challenging relationship.	Building Relationship Versatility Crucial Conversations 7 Habits of Highly Effective People	B or C: Crucial Conversations: Patterson B: Results Through Relationships: Takash
Developing Others	Mentor a Leader Talent High Potential for at least six months.	Heart-Centered Leadership Crucial Conversations Leading for Growth Talent Coaching	B or C – Gung Ho: Blanchard B-Heart-Centered Leadership: Steinbrecher
Strategic Thinking	Plan and lead a Strategy Session with your team. Serve on a Profit or Non-Profit Board of Directors for at least one year. Facilitate the course: Our Strategic Plan	Process Reality Leading for Growth	B or C - Good to Great: Collins E-Why Finance Matters Course
Customer Focus	Lead a focus group with customers for feedback. Conduct a customer feedback survey and identify areas of strength and improvement.	Process Reality Services Simulation	B or C: Raving Fans: Blanchard and Bowles Our Iceberg is Melting: Kotter
Innovation	Identify an area of process, service, or employee engagement improvement; sponsor and/or alead a project team	Leading in Challenging Times	B-The Heart of Change: Kotter B or C: Our Iceberg is Melting: Kotter E-Managing Change Course
Integrity	Working with your team of direct reports, identify actions you can take as their leader to build trust, and team strength – add this to your development plan.	7 Habits of Highly Effective People	B or C: The Speed of Trust

360 Actions	What will you do to leverage your Top Strength?	What will you do to improve your Top Development Need?
Career Growth Actions	Identify career path options with your leader:	What qualifications, experience and knowledge are needed?

How Do I Develop Employees On-the-Job?

Think about the opportunities you have received in your career which have prepared you for the position you hold today. Most likely, you received many on-the-job opportunities, as well as formal development resources.

 For your own employees, provide a similar combination of on-the-job development opportunities, new job assignments and formal development workshops and resources to create best practice development plans. As much as possible, create "two-way" development actions that provide business results for the organization and development results for employees.

Examples of these "two-way" development actions include:

Development Action	The Individual will build...	The organization...
Employees serve on critical project teams.	**...leadership skills, strategic thinking, cross-functional relationships and project management skills.**	**...benefits from having top talent contribute ideas and strategic thinking to the most critical issues.**
An employee takes a new lateral position in another function or department for development.	**...a wider breadth of knowledge, skills and experience, and wider network across the company.**	**...benefits by developing leaders with an enhanced understanding of the goals and issues faced by the different departments, functions and divisions of the company.**
Employees serve in mentor and/or training roles to others in the company to develop leadership skills.	**...the ability to develop others, to present information effectively, and to coach others.**	**...benefits from the training provided by experienced talent within the company, rather than always paying for external training resources.**

Development—Building Competencies

Even if we do a great job of setting goals, reviewing performance, and identifying successors and future talent needs, if we don't develop employees for success in both their current and future roles, we are missing a critical "follow-through" action.

Development begins with:

- **An Individual Development Plan (IDP) for each employee**

  OR

- **A New Employee Onboarding Plan for new employees**

The most effective development plans include both on-the-job learning experiences and the use of structured learning resources:

Examples of On-the-Job Development	Examples of Structured Development
• **Planned developmental lateral moves or job rotations to build new competencies** • **Promotion opportunities to build leadership and strategic ability** • **On-the-job stretch assignments and special projects to build new skills** • **New roles and responsibilities assigned within the employee's current job description and performance goals** • **Mentoring other employees** • **Working with a mentor to learn new competencies and new perspectives**	• **360-Degree Feedback and Coaching** • **Formal training workshops** • **Reading leadership books** • **E-learning courses** • **Higher education and degree course work** • **Obtaining certifications and licenses for specific skills** • **Attending external conferences and group seminar events**

Leadership Development Ideas—Be Creative!

Each employee should have an Individual Development Plan (IDP) that is discussed and updated during the year. Consider a variety of development options and remember that employees learn the most from on-the-job assignments, such as taking on a new job responsibility, serving on a new project team, or resolving a challenging issue.

 While some excellent development resources do require a budget, many of the best development ideas cost little or nothing other than an investment of time.

To obtain new knowledge, skills, and leadership experience, high potential leaders can:

Serve on a Project Team	Obtain 360 Feedback and Coaching
Participate in Leadership Workshops	Participate in a Leadership Book Club
Obtain an Executive Mentor or Sponsor	Present at an Industry Conference
Serve on a Non-Profit Board	Serve as a Community Service Leader
Obtain a Job Rotation Assignment	Publish in an Industry Periodical
Complete an E-Learning Course	Mentor New Employees
Develop Internal Procedure Guides	Develop / Deliver Internal Training
Complete a New Degree or MBA	Attend Industry Association Meetings
Participate in a Business Simulation	Take on a New Job Stretch Assignment
Join a Local Toastmasters Group	Participate in a Research Project
Obtain / Update a Certification	Work with an Executive Coach
Meet with the CEO or Board	Speak at the New Employee Orientation

Individual Development Plans

Today's Individual Development Plan (IDP) should provide ideas **both** to leverage strengths and to address competency gaps. Additionally, the IDP should pertain to **both** the employee's current position and to future career path options, to help increase readiness for the employee to move into new positions.

Current Role: Finance Manager	Potential Future Roles: Operations Manager, Finance Director, HR-Administration Manager	
	Enhancing Strengths	*Developing Gaps*
Development Actions for the Current Position	Identify metrics for new client program by end of first quarter. Present a lunch seminar for the Operations Managers on "Identifying Metrics for Business Results".	Attend the Conflict Management Workshop by end of 2nd quarter Work with HR to address conflicts in the work team to improve relationships and processes.
Development Actions for Next Potential Positions	Present the financial metrics and new budget to the Executive Team by end of first quarter.	Participate on the Performance Appraisal Revision project team.
360 Feedback and Development Actions	To leverage your strength of analyzing financial data, analyze each group's budget within our department, and make recommendations.	Needs to listen more and collaborate before making decisions—obtain strategic recommendations from each employee before developing executive recommendations.
Risk Management Actions	Document the monthly budget variance reporting process for the organization by end of second quarter.	

The development plan should also include **risk management actions**, which are designed to reduce company risk if and when the employee moves into a new position or leaves the organization. Examples of risk management actions can include developing successors, documenting procedures, mentoring others, providing workshops to share knowledge, etc.

Identifying high potentials but not actively developing them is like an Olympic coach identifying an amazing ice skating prodigy and then walking away. Exceptional results come only when raw talent is combined with practice, coaching and development.

Doris Sims Spies, SPHR